TOP 50 REAL FUNNY STORIES TO READ BEFORE YOU DIE

John Kang

WhatNowKorea

CONTENTS

INTRODUCTION

Top 50 Real Funny Stories To Read Before You Die

This book contains 50 of the most interesting stories in Korea. And these stories are all real things.

It's so funny that you might get dehydrated, so make sure to keep bottled water next to you.

What more can I say?

CHAPTER 1 : DEAD RABBIT

Suddenly, my dog barked for a long time.
The dog came in with a strange object... when I approached him,

"Huck!!! -_-; "

The white rabbit, which the daughters of the next door loved so much, was dead with a lot of dirt on it, and it was on my dog's mouth.

I felt my back sweating.

"Oh, how shall I do this... That damn dog...

The daughter of the next door loved the rabbit so much.
I decided to plan a complete crime...
It was a little gross. But I came into the house with a dead rabbit...
Wash until hair turns white in the bath...

First of all, I'll do that to get rid of the dirt.

I dried the rabbit's hair with a blow dryer.
Also, cleanly wash and dry the sky blue ribbon with dirt.
I tied it to the rabbit's body...

It was worth saying that she died naturally.
just across the fence There was no one in the yard next door. Jump over...

I put a dead rabbit in the rabbit house.
I came home as if nothing happened.

When I blame the dog for calling him a fucking bitch...
Next door... I hear screams...
Soon I could hear the hum of the voice...

I have no choice but to... I asked them what happened...

Their daughters and their uncle were all blue.
"The rabbit... the rabbit... "All I could say was ...
I felt guilty, but... pretend to be...

What about the rabbit? I asked him, "
Then he said,

..

..

..

"Some crazy guy.
 The rabbit died yesterday and buried it in the yard.
Some crazy guy washed it clean and put it back in the rabbit house...

CHAPTER 2 : CUTLET DELIVERY

I was pooping after ordering pork cutlet. I heard the ringtone, so I thought it was my mom.
I said, "I'm pooping!!!!!!!!!!!!!!!!!!!!!!!!!!!!!!! " outside the door.
"Well, the pork cutlet delivery is here. I'll wait for you outside."
He laughed when he got the money.

CHAPTER 3 : IN JJIM-JIL-BANG(KOREAN SAUNA)

I went to a Korean jjimjilbang with my mom and she said she was going to stay at a steam room.
I came out first, dressed up, and I was texting with my friend on the Daecheong floor.
A lady came to me and told me,

"You know how to text, don't you?" I'm not good at texting, so could you write for me?" And she gave me her phone.
So I took her phone and said, "Tell me what you want to send."

Then she suddenly gets excited and says to me...

"Hey, you son of a bitch. I know you're with her.
I'm going to call Detective Kim and go over there right now, you little fuck.
I'm gonna cut your throat."
Hehehehehehehehehehehehehehehehe.
In the meantime, I wrote it with trembling hands.

"You know, your cell phone is old, so I can only send 40 characters at a time."
So I sent it in two.

CHAPTER 4 : GOT A FART

I was playing computer in the living room, and I got a fart.

But it smelled so bad that I sprayed Parisian medicine.lol

That's when my brother came in and he said,
"She's farting again and again, she's spraying Parisian medicine.:"

I said, "My fart smells bad. Why?!!"

And after that, my brother's friends are coming in one afterLOL

CHAPTER 5 : PIGEONS

I had an appointment in the morning, but I was very late.
I don't usually run, but I just wanted to run once today.
There's a park in front of my house, and there's a lot of pigeon
magpie sparrows there.
There's a bunch of pigeons in front of the traffic lights.
The light turned blue and I ran at full speed.
I thought if I ran, the pigeons would be surprised and fly away.

That's a miscalculation.

I kicked a pigeon and it flew away.
a real fright
I can still feel the touch of that foot.
And when I turned around, there was a pigeon down.

There's a kid next to me crying.
It's awkward for her mother to tell her that pigeons are okay.

CHAPTER 6 : CONCEPTION DREAM

It's about my friend's brother's conception dream.

When she was sleeping, a black object was reflected by the sun in the clear sky.
They were flying around.
So she had a hard time catching it, and...

It was a black plastic bag.LOL
This is a preconventional dream.LOL

My friend who heard it was hilarious. He fell back.
My brother suddenly lost his mind.
LOL

CHAPTER 7 : LEE SUNG-JIN'S STORY

Celebrity Lee Sung-jin is popular in China.

So he went to China with the members.
It's so out of the way to go to the concert He had to take a plane.
But there was a light plane.
They said it was a really old light plane.

They were forced to ride it and the captain of the plane was a totally old grandfather....lol

But the old man suddenly said...LOL

I love flying. ...

My dream is to be on a plane and die.......................

CHAPTER 8 : MY COUSIN

I opened the door of my mom's room and it was locked.

I don't know what happens when I'm immature, and when I call her "Mom~," something rumbled inside.
After a while, the mother with the expression of her face came out and was very kind to me.

Phew...

after matured.
I don't even think about turning the handle when the door is locked.

Instead, my beloved cousin...

The day her mom and dad locked up...

When she was a sensitive 9th grader...LOL

with a frantic knock on the door
"Come
out!!
!
I know what you're doing.
What the hell are you doing?"

She said, "Hahahahahaha.

CHAPTER 9 : FUNNY WHEN SURGERY

I was really funny when I had surgery.
While the doctor was operating, the nurse said, "Teacher, you have an important call.Take it for a second."
Even in that delirious state of mind,
"Don't you focus on my nose?" he says.
The doctor laughed so hard that he came back and focused. Hehe-hehehehehehehehehehehehehehehehe.

The doctor said, "Is sleep anesthesia still under control? The patient is out of his mind."

During the entire operation, I kept telling the doctor, "Fighting, fighting, hahaha."
Anyway, I never want to lie on the table again. Phew. It's like hell

Halton, I never want to lie on the table again. Phew. It's like hell.

CHAPTER 10 : GENIUS

It happened when I was in 2nd grade in elementary school. I pretended to be a genius. So I pretended to read science books every day and secretly read books like "The Outcast of the Rings" at home.
One day a friend came to me and said, "I have a sore on my tongue." So I don't even know what it is, but I'm going to pretend I know. "sore? I got it last year and it's all better if I stick it with a needle. I'll ask my mom to buy that needle, so don't worry!" And all the kids there clapped and said, "Wow! Suny(=my name) knows everything. It's the best!"
So when I got home, I proudly said, "Mom, give me a needle so I can cure my friend"
Mom smiles and tells me "No"

But the next day, I went to school, and all my classmates came to see me.
I was thinking, "What Should I do?"
Just lightly touch the tongue with the thread at the back of the needle and say, "Oh, I'm finally. If you had a little more of this, it would have spread to cancer."
So all the kids around gave me a standing ovation and said, "Suny is a real doctor! Doctor!"

He wiped off his sweat with a look on his face as if he had been cured of a deadly disease, and said, "Suny, I would have been in the hospital without you."

Ah, I would be a real fool in their memories. Please, forget it.

CHAPTER 11 : INCORRECT TEXT MESSAGE TO TEACHER

Incorrect text message to teacher

I was texting with my friend and my homeroom teacher because of college entrance.
I was going to send a friend, "I'm getting a poop signal. Attention, low!"
But I sent it to my homeroom teacher.

I got a reply.
"I like this friendly relationship. Make yourself at home and fill in the application form. Fun poop!"

My homeroom teacher is 28 years old and a first male teacher.

CHAPTER 12 : SONG JOONG-KI (FAN MEETING) LEE KWANG-SOO ANECDOTE

Song Joong-ki (fan meeting) Lee Kwang-soo anecdote

When Lee Kwang-soo held the microphone to say goodbye for the last time, fans shouted, "Don't go."
Then what Lee Kwang-soo says.

"I have a job, too. My job is not a BTS friend."

CHAPTER 13 : WHY MY DAD DOESN'T GO TO CHURCH

Why my dad doesn't go to church

His baptismal name is "Titto."
His grandmother built it under duress.

CHAPTER 14 : A CREEPY EXPERIENCE WITH ME AND MY FRIEND.

A creepy experience with me and my friend.

My friend and I went to the reading room together.
It was exam period, so I studied in the reading room until 1 a.m. and came out to go home.

But get hungry when get out at one. So we went to the tteokbokki place for 24 hours and settled down by the window.

But when I was chatting with my friend, he turned pale looking at the window and pointed his finger at the window

So I looked at the window, "What is it?"

Me and my friend are passing by.
The face, clothes, and hair were all the same.

So I watched it blankly. They saw us, too.
They were all stiff at us, too. And all of a sudden, they were running.

My friend and I screamed, cried, and I was so scared.
It was when I was in the 9th grade and I still remember it.

CHAPTER 15 : MATH

Primary Math: It's impossible to subtract 200 from 100.
Secondary Math: If you squared, you can't get negative numbers.
Advanced Math: It's actually all possible. Idiots.
University: Now prove it to me.
Company: What math is it is? Don't talk rubbish. Go get this copy.

CHAPTER 16 : HIGH TENSION IN CLASS

High tension in class

I was told to stop clicking on the pen.
the tension of having to press once more to write the pen

CHAPTER 17 : MIMICKED THE CA

I mimicked the cat in the alley with many cats. But, unlike usual, cats answered.
I was so excited that I was "meow meow" the whole way.

Suddenly, I heard a sound from over there saying, "Wow, that's a real answer."

I found out that I had exchanged cat sounds with an unknown person.

CHAPTER 18 : TWO GINSENG

Yesterday, my brother's friend was caught by his brother because he was drunk.

I didn't even know my brother was coming from the living room, so I was wearing a yellow underwear with my mom. When my brother and his friend came, I was surprised and ran away.

next day
My brother friend said that he went to your house and saw ginseng.

I don't know if it's a dream, but the ginsengs are just going around. They were both years of fat ginseng.

CHAPTER 19 : OLD BUS

I took a bus and it was kind of an old bus.
I sat on the left side of the back seat and there was a man sitting on the other end of me.
It was shaking a lot because it was an old bus.
However, the bus driver did not see the bump while running, so the bus jumped.
I hit my head on the ceiling because I was at the end.
I thought some degree of shock had cracked my skull.
I was so sick that I couldn't pretend to be not sick
I looked at the man on the other side.

The ceiling is broken lol

CHAPTER 20 : PERSONAL INSTRUMENT

The teacher asked me to bring a personal instrument.
But I forgot to bring it.
Because the music teacher was very scary, I didn't think it would end with a score cut. So I took out the air cushion and opened it like castanets.

The teacher tried to scold me, but I continued with an iron plate on my face.
Then my teacher told me to play with an air cushion until I had a performance assessment.

CHAPTER 21 : SAD NIGHTMARE

I wasn't scared, I had a rather sad nightmare.

I was taking a nap on a rainy day, but I felt quite sober that day. So I just try to get up, but my body doesn't move.

"Oh, this is a nightmare," I thought.

 I'm trying to figure out how to solve it, and the problem has been since then. Someone hits the door lock and enters the house.

But his shoes seemed to be full of water. There was a thud as he walked.

The sound of the men's shoes drew closer to my room.

I was really very, very scared. But the man sat by my bedside. I couldn't see the man's face because I slept with the blanket up to my head.

How long has it been?

The man spoke. His voice was just a middle-aged man.

"I miss my daughter.

There's so much I couldn't do for you. So I'm so sorry. Will you forgive me?"

I got emotional thinking about my dad. So I was listening carefully.

Then he suddenly stood up.

"I'm sorry. I missed my daughter so much. But I couldn't see you, so I came looking for you who look like my daughter. This is the last time I'll say something, thinking it's my daughter."

And then...

"Be healthy. My daughter's dad loves you."

And the real nightmare was over. And I cried because I was so sad.

CHAPTER 22 : REALLY RECOGNIZES ME

I was told from the morning, "Do you not want to work?" I'm working with my boss who really recognizes me.

CHAPTER 23 : MY FRIEND'S NAME IS KIM JONG UN.

My friend's name is Kim Jong Un.

But while eating, He was short of rice.
I told my friends around me
"Kim Jong-un needs more rice."
Friend said. "Why? Another missile?"

That day, My friends did everything to cheer him up.

CHAPTER 24 : ROBOT VACUUM CLEANER.

I was cleaning the house with a robot vacuum cleaner.

He disappeared in the elevator.

Where did you go?

CHAPTER 25 : PROPOSE

Someone was preparing to propose with his sister.
But He drank so much that He fell asleep.
So, while His sister was preparing for it, His girlfriend suddenly came in.
So His sister said, "Can you be my new sister?"

CHAPTER 26 : MY MEAN DOG

The funny thing about my dog is,
When he farts, he smells my ass.
The dog is very mean.

CHAPTER 27 : LIFT UP YOUR ASS

I am on the subway now.

The man next to me sat on my coat and tried to take it out, but it didn't come off.
I said, "Please, lift up your ass."
He said, "No."
So I'm just on my way.

CHAPTER 28 : SQUID

I ordered rice topped with squid in the restaurant.
The lady said, "Who's the squid?"
I said, "Me"
but something upset me.

CHAPTER 29 : GIFT TO DAD

I bought him a sweater for his birthday. Dad tore open the package and didn't react much.

He didn't even say thank you.
I didn't expect it from the start, so I didn't feel bad.

The next week, my parents went on a trip with other couples for two weeks.

Mom showed me the picture taken after the trip.

Clearly, Mom's clothes have changed, but Dad's clothes haven't changed at all.

Every picture was wearing the clothes I bought for him.

CHAPTER 30 : INTERVIEW

I had an interview at a university to find out my English proficiency.
ciency.
"Use conversation with the professor in front of you to get directions to Seoul Station."
Student : Where are you from?
Professor : I'm from korea
Student: Nice to meet you. Please speak in Korean.

CHAPTER 31 : MY LIFE IS SO STUPID.

My life is so stupid.

I wish someone would slap me on the cheek.
But if you slap me in the face, I will kill you.

CHAPTER 32 : SHE CRIES

I'm a part-timer at a convenience store.
I was displaying the items and a male elementary school student came in and walked to the counter.
The elementary student suddenly said, "You look like a old lady walking."
Then I said, "Then you breathe like an old man."
So suddenly she cries.

CHAPTER 33 : CHECK THE TREES

I was sleeping with my boyfriend for about 2 months.
But in the middle, I got stuck in the fart. It was the biggest ever.
I farted and opened my eyes in surprise. My boyfriend jumped up from his sleep.
I was pretending to sleep because I was embarrassed. And then my boyfriend shook me up.
"I think the tree is split in front of my house."
So I pretended to be surprised and went to the yard with him to check the trees.

CHAPTER 34 : MY FATHER

Someone's father came in drunk at night.
He put his left foot on the sink to wash his feet.
And he looked at his right foot, and he said, "Oh, I'm going to put this foot on it."
He was taken to the hospital while raising his right foot.

CHAPTER 35 : GET OUT!

had a fight with my husband last night.

I told my husband, "Now take as much as you can and get out." Then he lifted me up and went out the door.

CHAPTER 36 : HEARING AID

Two old men were sitting in a chair and talking.
An old man opened his mouth first.
"Hey, I bought a new hearing aid. It's very expensive."
The other old man envied and said, "So how much is it?"

The old man looked at his watch and answered.
"12 o'clock"

CHAPTER 37 : GRANDMOTHER AND DRIVER

Grandmother and driver

The bus's buzzer is out of order.
An old lady went quietly to the driver and said just one word.

"Beep~"

CHAPTER 38 : A PREGNANT LADY

A pregnant lady

The baby girl met a pregnant lady next door. asked the girl.

"Why are you full?"
The lady replied. "Yes, it's because there's a pretty baby in it."

Then the baby girl said,

"How did you end up eating your baby?"

CHAPTER 39 : THE WIFE ASKED HER HUSBAND.

The wife asked her husband.
"Was there a girl you were dating before wedding? Tell me the truth."

"Yes, I did."

"Really? Did you love her?"

"Yes, I loved her hot."

"Have you ever kissed?"

"I've tried."

My wife finally got angry.

"Do you still love her?"

"Then I love her. It's my first love..."

My wife is totally angry. Then she screamed.

"Why didn't you marry her, then?"

Then husband said,

"So I married her."

CHAPTER 40 : SUN OF MY LIFE

Girl: Be the sun of my life
Man: Oh! Okay.
Girl: Can you now get 150 million kilometers away from me?

CHAPTER 41 : ANGELINUS WANTED

There was an event in the coffee shop called "Angelinus" that offered half price discount if you ordered coffee with an angel accent.

ANGELINUS Wanted: Can I have a nice cup of Americano? Thank you very much.

People: Oh Michael, I ran from heaven to find you. I'm so thirsty. Serve me a drink of life made of sacred fruit in a large cup.

CHAPTER 42 : ARE YOU CRAZY?

He was standing at the bus stop, touching his phone.
But someone keeps hitting him in the back.
At first, He stayed still. But someone kept hitting, so he loudly.
"Are you crazy? do you want to get hit?" he looked back.
It was a branch

He took any bus because he feel like fish out of water.

CHAPTER 43 : WHEN I WAS IN PUBERTY.

It happened when I was in puberty.
Mom came into my room.
So I told my mom, "Don't barge into my room!"
My mother was so serious that she said, "Don't barge into my house."
Mom kicked me out of the gate.

CHAPTER 44 : I LIKED THE MAN WHO WORKED AT THE GAS STATION

I liked the man who worked at the gas station by myself.
So I bought a liter of gasoline every day.
One day there was a chain fire in the neighborhood, and the police were going around investigating.
The part-timer named me the primary suspect to the police.

CHAPTER 45 : A MONK AND A LITTLE MONK

It's a cute thing that just happened.
A monk and a little monk came into the cafe and ordered iced chocolate.
As it was hard for the little monk to wait, he cried and asked me, "When is ours coming out?"

And I said, "There's an order in everything. Little Monk."
Then the little monk said, "Huck!" And he went to the monk, and he said, "I see a Buddha in her heart."

CHAPTER 46 : BLIND DATE.

My stomach started to ache when I was on a blind date.
So I told the guy honestly that I had a stomachache.

Then the man spoke very gently.
"It's my house a little further. Do you want to poop?"

CHAPTER 47 : MEAT RESTAURANT

I went to the meat restaurant which I went several times during lunch time.
There was a new part-timer.
The part-timer approached me and said, "I'm sorry. We don't sell one serving."

Then the owner came out and said, "This lady eats two servings"
He insulted part-timer and told me not to worry.

CHAPTER 48 : I KISSED MY BOYFRIEND

When I was in high school, I kissed my boyfriend, and he was the first to kiss.
My boyfriend didn't support my back of my neck. So it was so hard.
So I grabbed the back of my neck by myself.

CHAPTER 49 : I THOUGHT NOBODY WAS HOME.

I thought nobody was home.
As soon as I got home, I hugged my dog, sang "Let it go," and I sat him on the couch.

And I'll act like this way.
"Oh, I'm sorry, brother. I'm late for cancer. I'm sorry. Be happy...."

Take my note out of the bag, put on my mom's high heels, walk to the puppy,
"Sir, this afternoon's schedule. You have a dinner appointment with the Samsung chairman."
I'm drawing a line on my notebook like this way.

Suddenly the door opened, and my brother, father, and friend came out clapping.

 I left the house right away. I came to my friend's house after eating ramen at the convenience store in front of my house.

 I think I can't go home

CHAPTER 50 : WHAT'S YOUR NAME?

A college ornithology department took a test, pasting a picture of a bird's leg and guessing what it was.

One student said, "Professor, isn't this too much? The test is weird."

So the professor said, "What's your name?"

Then the student sticks out one leg and says, "Let's guess."

www.ingramcontent.com/pod-product-compliance
Lightning Source LLC
Chambersburg PA
CBHW031241130726
47988CB00008B/3184